Quick Reference Guide

INTRODUCTORY Lotus 1·2·3™
IBM PC

is Blanc/Elinore J. Hildebrandt

Dictation Disc Company

First Dictation Disc Printing May 1989

ISBN: 0-936862-31-9

10   9   8   7

Printed in the United States of America

TABLE OF CONTENTS

© 1986 Dictation Disc Company
14 East 38 Street, New York, NY 10016

Introduction

This quick reference guide to LOTUS 1-2-3™ is correlated to
SPREADSHEETS: APPLICATIONS AND EXERCISES. Only those
features covered in the book's applications are outlined in this
guide.

Illustrations of the LOTUS 1-2-3™ worksheet and menu maps
have been provided on pages c-j to help you locate desired
commands. A template for the IBM PC (and compatibles)
function keys has been outlined on page k for you to cut out
and place over those keys.

The table of contents appears on the front cover of this
booklet. An index, referencing all commands and functions
covered in the booklet, appears on the back cover.

It is our hope that this booklet will help you to use LOTUS
1-2-3™ effortlessly.

Iris Blanc
Ellie Hildebrandt

b

Illustration of a Lotus Spreadsheet

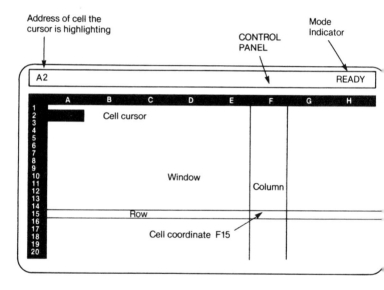

Address of cell the cursor is highlighting

CONTROL PANEL

Mode Indicator

A2 READY

Cell cursor

Window

Column

Row

Cell coordinate F15

c

Lotus 1-2-3™ Main Menu

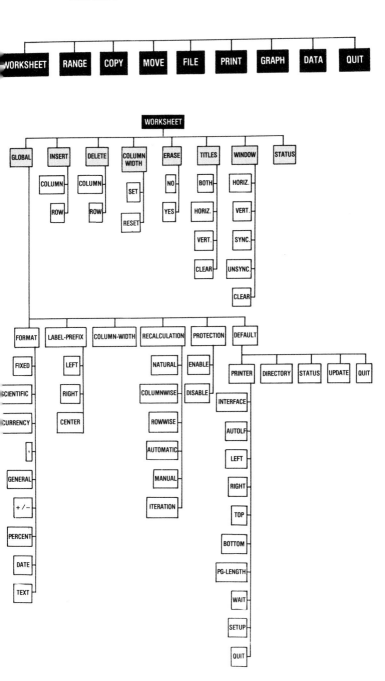

d

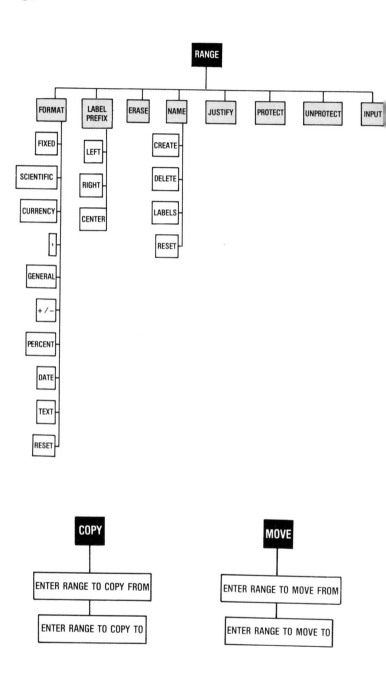

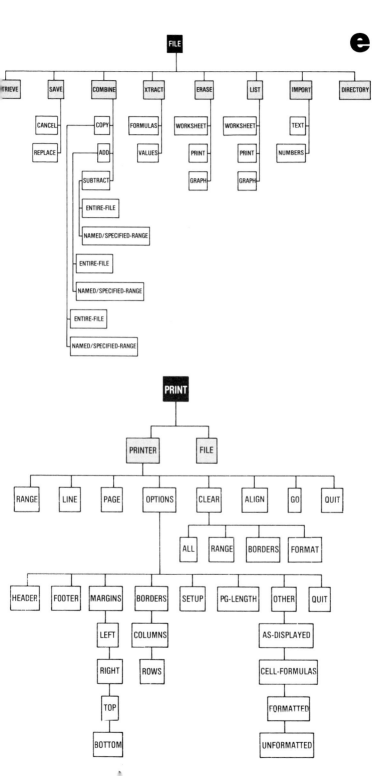

FILE   **e**

- RETRIEVE
- SAVE
  - CANCEL
  - REPLACE
- COMBINE
  - COPY
    - ENTIRE-FILE
    - NAMED/SPECIFIED-RANGE
  - ADD
    - ENTIRE-FILE
    - NAMED/SPECIFIED-RANGE
  - SUBTRACT
    - ENTIRE-FILE
    - NAMED/SPECIFIED-RANGE
- XTRACT
  - FORMULAS
  - VALUES
- ERASE
  - WORKSHEET
  - PRINT
  - GRAPH
- LIST
  - WORKSHEET
  - PRINT
  - GRAPH
- IMPORT
  - TEXT
  - NUMBERS
- DIRECTORY

PRINT

- PRINTER
  - RANGE
  - LINE
  - PAGE
  - OPTIONS
    - HEADER
    - FOOTER
    - MARGINS
      - LEFT
      - RIGHT
      - TOP
      - BOTTOM
    - BORDERS
      - COLUMNS
      - ROWS
    - SETUP
    - PG-LENGTH
    - OTHER
      - AS-DISPLAYED
      - CELL-FORMULAS
      - FORMATTED
      - UNFORMATTED
    - QUIT
  - CLEAR
    - ALL
    - RANGE
    - BORDERS
    - FORMAT
  - ALIGN
  - GO
  - QUIT
- FILE

f

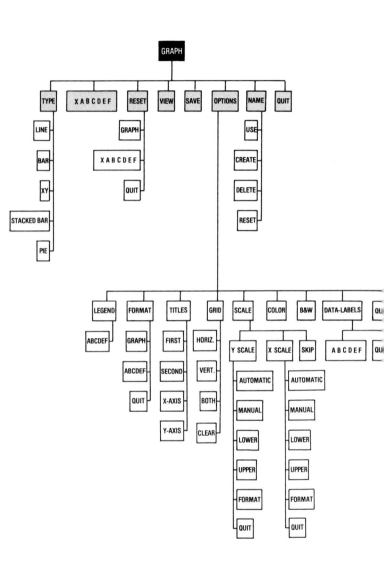

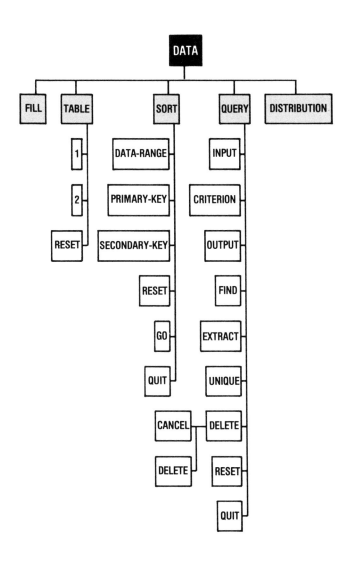

Template

CUT OUT TEMPLATE ALONG DOTTED LINE

LOTUS 1-2-3

HELP	EDIT
NAME	ABS
GOTO	WINDOW
QUERY	TABLE
CALC	GRAPH

← CUT OUT →
TEMPLATE
ALONG
DOTTED
LINE

Startup Procedure / Loading

For two floppy-disk drives.

1. Load the <u>System Disk</u> into Drive A.
2. Close the door.
3. Load the <u>Data Disk</u> into Drive B.
4. Close the door.
5. Turn the computer on.
6. Type the <u>date</u> (XX-XX-XX).
7. ENTER.
8. Type the <u>time</u> (XX:XX).
9. ENTER.
10. Type LOTUS at the A>.
11. ENTER.
12. Highlight 1-2-3.
13. ENTER.
14. Strike any key.

For a hard-disk drive with one floppy-disk drive.

1. Turn the computer on.
2. Type the <u>date</u> (XX-XX-XX).
3. ENTER.
4. Type the <u>time</u> (XX:XX).
5. ENTER.
6. Load the <u>Data Disk</u> into Drive A.
7. Close the door.
8. Type LOTUS at the C>.
9. ENTER.
10. Highlight 1-2-3.
11. ENTER.
12. Strike any key.

2

Exploring the Spreadsheet

Cursor movements

To move : Right .... `→`

Left .... `←`

Down .... `↓`

Up .... `↑`

Screen Page Down .... `PgDn`

Screen Page Up .... `PgUp`

Screen Page Right .... `Tab`

Screen Page Left .... `Shift` + `Tab`

Directly to a Cell

1. Depress GOTO .... `F5`
2. Type cell address.
3. Depress ENTER .... `↵`

Starting Position .... `Home`

Bottom Right Edge of Worksheet .. `End` + `Home`

Left Edge of a List .... `End` + `←`

Right Edge of a List .... `End` + `→`

Top of a List .... `End` + `↑`

Bottom of a List .... `End` + `↓`

Entering Labels

NOTE: The mode indicator must say READY.

ALPHABETIC

1. Place cursor in desired cell.
2. Type a label.
3. ENTER or depress a cursor arrow key in the direction of the next entry.*

*NOTE: Labels will automatically left-justify after entry.

To center or right justify a label, see page 20.

NUMERIC

(Numeric labels **will not** calculate)

1. Place cursor in desired cell.
2. Type an apostrophe (Label-Prefix).**
3. Type label.
4. ENTER or depress a cursor arrow key in the direction of the next entry.

**NOTE: Using an apostrophe as a label prefix will left justify the numeric label. To center or right justify a numeric label, see page 20.

4

Storing / Saving
A new worksheet

1. Depress HOME.
2. Type / (Menu)............................ `/`
3. Type F (File)............................ `F`
4. Type S (Save)........................... `S`
5. Type a file name.
6. ENTER .... `↵`

Re-Storing / Re-Saving
Overwriting a worksheet

1. Depress HOME.
2. Type / (Menu)............................ `/`
3. Type F (File)............................ `F`
4. Type S (Save)........................... `S`
5. ENTER .... `↵`
6. Type R (Replace)........................ `R`

Clearing / Erasing

Screen / Worksheet

1. Type / (Menu).................................. ⬛/

2. Type W (Worksheet)......................... ⬛W

3. Type E (Erase)............................... ⬛E

4. Type Y (Yes)................................. ⬛Y

A cell or range of cells

1. Move cursor to the first cell
   to be erased.

2. Type / (Menu).................................. ⬛/

3. Type R (Range)............................... ⬛R

4. Type E (Erase)............................... ⬛E

5. Highlight cell or range of cells
   to be erased.

6. ENTER .... ⬛↵

Recalling/Retrieving

1. Type / (Menu) .... ▨

2. Type F (File) .... **F**

3. Type R (Retrieve) .... **R**

4. Highlight file name to be retrieved using the cursor arrow keys.

5. ENTER .... ⏎

Entering Values

NOTE: • The mode indicator must say READY.

   • Do not use a comma, a dollar sign or a space in a value entry.

1. Place cursor in desired cell.

2. Type a value.

3. ENTER or depress a cursor arrow key in the direction of the next entry.

Entering Formulas

Using arithmetic symbols

1. Place cursor in the cell where answer should appear.
2. Type + (Plus) to put Lotus into VALUE MODE .... **+**
3. Move cursor to the first cell to be calculated.
4. Type desired arithmetic symbol: .... Option
    + (addition)   * (multiplication)
    – (subtraction)   / (division)
5. Move cursor to the next cell to be calculated.
   Repeat steps 4 & 5 if further calculations are necessary.
6. ENTER .... **↵**

Using built-in functions

1. Place cursor in the cell where answer should appear.
2. Type @ ("at" Symbol) .... **@**
3. Type name of the desired function: .... Option
    SUM (addition)   COUNT (count)
    MAX (maximum)   AVG   (average)
    MIN (minimum)
4. Type ((Open Parenthesis) .... **(**
5. Move cursor to first cell to be calculated.
6. Type . (Period) to lock in the range .... **·**
7. Move cursor to the last cell in the range
   to be calculated. (The range will be highlighted)
8. Type) (Closed Parenthesis) .... **)**
9. ENTER .... **↵**

8

Entering Formulas
For absolute conditions

NOTE: Absolute symbols must be used to indicate
a no-change condition WHEN COPYING formulas.

Using arithmetic symbols

1. Place cursor in the cell where the answer
   should appear.

2. Type + (Plus) to put Lotus into VALUE MODE...... **[+]**

3. Move cursor to the first cell to be calculated.

4. Type F4 (Absolute) to indicate a no-change
   condition .... **[F4]**

5. Type desired arithmetic symbol: .... Option
   + (addition)   * (multiplication)   **[+*]**
   − (subtraction)   / (division)   **[−/]**

6. Move cursor to the next cell to be calculated.

7. Type F4 (Absolute) to indicate a no change
   condition .... **[F4]**
   Repeat steps 4 - 5 if further calculations
   are necessary.

8. ENTER .... **[↵]**

Entering Formulas continued —

Using built-in functions

1. Place cursor in the cell where the answer should appear.

2. Type @ ("at" Symbol) .... `@`

3. Type name of the desired function:............ **Option**
   - SUM (addition)   COUNT (count)
   - MAX (maximum)   AVG   (average)
   - MIN (minimum)

4. Type ((Open Parenthesis) .... `(`

5. Move cursor to the first cell to be calculated.

6. Type F4 (Absolute) to indicate a no change condition .... `F4`

7. Type . (Period) to lock in the range............... `.`

8. Move cursor to the last cell in the range to be calculated. (The range will be highlighted)

9. Type F4 (Absolute) to indicate a no-change condition... `F4`

10. Type) (Closed Parenthesis) .... `)`

11. ENTER .... `↵`

Copying

A cell, a range of cells, or a formula
(See pages 8-9 to create an absolute condition.)

1. Move cursor to the first cell to be copied.

2. Type / (Menu).. `/`

3. Type C (Copy).. `C`

4. Highlight cell or range of cells to
   be copied FROM.

5. ENTER .... `⏎`

6. Move cursor to the first cell
   to be copied TO.

7. Type . (Period) to lock in the range.............. `.`

8. Highlight cell or range of cells to
   be copied TO.

9. ENTER .... `⏎`

Printing

1. Move cursor to the first cell to be printed.

2. Type / (Menu).. `/`

3. Type P (Print)....................................... `P`

4. Type P (Printer)..................................... `P`

5. Type R (Range) .... `R`

6. Type . (Period) to lock in the range.............. `·`

7. Highlight range to be printed.

8. ENTER .... `↵`

9. Type A (Align)....................................... `A`

10. Type G (Go).. `G`

11. Type Q (Quit) .... `Q`

12

Printing / Compressed

1. Move cursor to the first cell to be printed.
2. Type / (Menu) .... `/`
3. Type P (Print) .... `P`
4. Type P (Printer) .... `P`
5. Type R (Range) .... `R`
6. Type . (Period) to lock in the range .... `·`
7. Highlight range to be printed
8. ENTER .... `↵`
9. Type O (Options) .... `O`
10. Type M (Margins) .... `M`
11. Type R (Right) .... `R`
12. Type 132 (for standard 80-column printer) or 240 (for a wide-column printer)
13. ENTER .... `↵`
14. Type S (Setup) .... `S`

Printing / Compressed continued

Printing / Compressed (continued)

15. Type \ (Backslash) .... ◣

16. Type Setup String (refer to <u>printer manual</u>
    for appropriate code) .... SetUp String

17. ENTER .... ↵

18. Type Q (Quit).. Q

19. Type A (Align)....................................... A

20. Type G (Go)... G

21. Type Q (Quit)....................................... Q

14

Inserting / Deleting Columns and Rows

Columns

1. Place cursor in the COLUMN where the insertion or deletion is to occur.
2. Type / (Menu)... `/`
3. Type W (Worksheet)............................... `W`
4. Type I (Insert) or Type D (Delete)......... `I` or `D`
5. Type C (Column)..................................... `C`
6. ENTER for one blank column .... `↵`
        or
   Highlight across for desired number of columns to be inserted or deleted and ENTER.

Rows

1. Place cursor in the ROW where the insertion or deletion is to occur.
2. Type / (Menu)... `/`
3. Type W (Worksheet)............................... `W`
4. Type I (Insert) or Type D (Delete)......... `I` or `D`
5. Type R (Row)... `R`
6. ENTER for one blank row .... `↵`
        or
   Highlight down for desired number of rows to be inserted or deleted and ENTER.

Fixing / Freezing Titles

1. Place cursor one ROW below or one COLUMN to right of where the freeze is to occur.

2. Type / (Menu)......................................

3. Type W (Worksheet)...........................

4. Type T (Titles)...................................

5. Select an option for splitting screen: .... Option
         B (Both)
         H (Horizontal)
         V (Vertical)

Clearing Title Freeze

1. Follow steps 2 - 4 above ....

2. Type C (Clear)...................................

Moving

**A cell or a range of cells
(including columns and rows) to a blank area.**

1. Move cursor to the first cell
   to be moved.

2. Type / (Menu) .... ▣

3. Type M (Move) .... **M**

4. Highlight cell or range of cells
   to be moved FROM.

5. ENTER .... ↵

6. Move cursor to the first cell in the
   range to be moved TO.

7. ENTER .... ↵

Drawing Lines

Horizontal

NOTE: This procedure may be used for repeating any character **within** a cell.

1. Place cursor in the cell where the horizontal line is to begin.

2. Type \ (Backslash) to activate the repeat action ....

3. Type - (Hyphen) or = (Equal) or any other desired character ....

4. ENTER ....

5. To copy the line to another cell or range of cells, use the copy procedure (see page 10).

Vertical

1. Adjust column to desired width (see page 19).

2. Place cursor in the cell where the vertical line is to begin.

3. Type ¦ (Vertical Line) or any other desired character ....

4. ENTER ....

5. To copy the line to another cell or range of cells, use the copy procedure (see page 10).

Editing

Strikeover correction

1. Place cursor in the cell to be edited.
2. Retype the entry.
3. ENTER.

Editing an existing cell entry

NOTE: If an error is made during editing process
before ENTER is depressed, depress ESC
(Escape) and entry will remain unchanged.

1. Place cursor in the cell to be edited.

2. Depress F2 (Edit) **F2**

3. Use edit keys to make corrections: .... **Option**

    To move cursor left and right .... **←** **→**

    To move cursor five characters to right .... **Tab**

    To move cursor five characters to left ..... **Shift** **Tab**

    To move cursor to the beginning of edit line .... **Home**

    To move cursor to the end of edit line .... **End**

    To delete character to left of cursor .... **Backspace**

    To delete character under cursor .... **Del**

4. ENTER .... **↵**

Setting Column Width

NOTE: Setting of a single column takes
precedence over a global setting.

Single column setting

1. Place cursor in the column to be changed.

2. Type / (Menu) .... `/`

3. Type W (Worksheet) .... `W`

4. Type C (Column-Width) .... `C`

5. Type S (Set) .... `S`

6. Depress right cursor arrow to desired
   column width .... `→`
         or
   Type the number of desired column width.

7. ENTER .... `↵`

Global column setting

1. Place cursor anywhere on the worksheet.

2. Type / (Menu) .... `/`

3. Type W (Worksheet) .... `W`

4. Type G (Global) .... `G`

5. Type C (Column-Width) .... `C`

6. Depress right cursor arrow to desired
   column width .... `→`
         or
   Type the number of desired column width.

7. ENTER .... `↵`

20

Formatting/Label Alignment

Before cell entry (left, right or center)

1. Place cursor in desired cell.
2. Type a label-prefix: .... Option
   - ' (Left Justify)
   - ∧ (Center)
   - " (Right Justify)
3. Type a label.
4. ENTER or depress a cursor arrow key in the direction of the next entry ....

After cell entry (left, right or center)

1. Place the cursor in desired cell.
2. Type / (Menu) ....
3. Type R (Range) ....
4. Type L (Label) ....
5. Select the desired alignment: .... Option
   - L (Left)
   - R (Right)
   - C (Center)
6. ENTER for single-cell alignment
   or
   highlight the range of cells to be
   aligned and ENTER ....

Formatting / Numeric

Local

1. Place cursor in the first cell where the desired format should appear.

2. Type / (Menu) .... **/**

3. Type R (Range) .... **R**

4. Type F (Format) .... **F**

5. Select a desired format: .... Option

   F (Fixed)   , (Comma)   **F ,**
   C (Currency)   P (Percent)   **C P**

6. Type desired number of decimal places (0 to 15)

7. ENTER for single formatting
          or
   highlight the range of cells to be
   formatted and ENTER .... **↵**

Global

1. Place cursor anywhere on the worksheet.

2. Type / (Menu) .... **/**

3. Type W (Worksheet) .... **W**

4. Type G (Global) .... **G**

5. Type F (Format) .... **F**

6. Select a desired format: .... Option

   F (Fixed)   , (Comma)   **F ,**
   C (Currency)   P (Percent)   **C P**

7. Type desired number of decimal places (0 to 15)

8. ENTER .... **↵**

Windows

1. Place cursor one ROW below or one COLUMN to the right of where the split is to occur.
2. Type / (Menu) .... **/**
3. Type W (Worksheet)................................... **W**
4. Type W (Window)...................................... **W**
5. Select an option for splitting the screen: .... **Option**
   - H (Horizontal)
   - V (Vertical)

NOTE: Depress F6 to move from one window to the other.

Synchronized / Unsynchronized Scrolling

1. Follow steps 2 - 5 above .... **/** **W** **W** **Option**
2. Type S (Sync) or U (Unsync)................... **S** or **U**

Clearing the Window

1. Follow steps 2 - 4 above .... **/** **W** **W**
2. Type C (Clear).. **C**

Lookup

1. Place cursor in the cell where the answer should appear.
2. Depress @ ("at" Symbol) .... `@`
3. Type name of the desired function .... **Option**
   VLOOKUP   (Vertical Lookup)
   HLOOKUP   (Horizontal Lookup)
4. Type ((Open Parenthesis) .... `(`
5. Type the search item cell address.
   or
   Move cursor to the cell that contains the search item.
6. Type , (Comma) .... `,`
7. Move cursor to the first cell in the table.
8. Type . (Period) to lock in the range .... `.`
9. Highlight the entire table.
10. Type , (Comma) .... `,`
11. Type a number that represents the column or row number of the table where the data to be returned lies.
    NOTE: First column or row in the table is always 0.
12. Type) (Closed Parenthesis) .... `)`
13. ENTER .... `↵`

Graphing

1. Retrieve worksheet from which graph is to be created.

2. Type / (Menu) .... **/**

3. Type G (Graph) .... **G**

4. Type T (Type) .... **T**

5. Select desired type of graph: .... Option
   - L   (Line)
   - B   (Bar)
   - S   (Stacked-Bar)
   - P   (Pie)

   L B / S P

6. Type X (to set X-axis data range) .... **X**

7. Move cursor to first cell in range to be scaled.

8. Type . (Period) to lock in the range .... **.**

9. Highlight the range of cells to be scaled.

10. ENTER .... **↵**

11. Type A (to set first Y-axis data range) .... **A**

12. Move cursor to first cell in range to be scaled.

13. Type . (Period) to lock in the range .... **.**

14. Highlight range of cells to be scaled.

15. ENTER .... **↵**

16. Repeat steps 11 – 15 for additional variables.
    To set additional data ranges:
        type B to set second data range;
        type C to set third data range, etc.

Graphing Options

Creating a legend

NOTE: If already working in the graphing submenu,
steps 1 and 2 below need not be repeated.

1. Type / (Menu) .... `/`

2. Type G (Graph)... `G`

3. Type O (Options) .... `O`

4. Type L (Legend) .... `L`

5. Type A (to name first Y-axis legend) .... `A`

6. Type a name for the first legend.

7. ENTER .... `↵`

8. Repeat steps 4-7 until all legend names have been entered.

Creating titles / headings

NOTE: If already working in the graphing submenu,
steps 1 and 2 below need not be repeated.

1. Type / (Menu) .... `/`

2. Type G (Graph) .... `G`

3. Type O (Options) ....

4. Type T (Titles) .... `T`

5. Type F (First) .... `F`

6. Type a name for the title or heading.

7. ENTER .... `↵`

8. Repeat steps 4-7 if a subtitle is desired.
At step 5 type S (Second).

Viewing Graphs

NOTE: If already working in the graphing submenu,
steps 1 and 2 below need not be repeated.

Procedure I

1. Type / (Menu) .... `/`

2. Type G (Graph) .... `G`

3. Type V (View) .... `V`

4. Depress ESC (Escape) to exit to graph menu ...... `Esc`

Procedure II

While in READY MODE, depress
F10 (Graph Key) .... `F10`

Saving Graphs

NOTE: •If already working in the graphing submenu,
steps 1 and 2 below need not be repeated.

•Graph image will be saved for **printing only**.

1. Type / (Menu) .... `/`

2. Type G (Graph) .... `G`

3. Type S (Save) .... `S`

4. Type graph file name.

5. ENTER .... `↵`

Naming Graph Settings for Recall

NOTE: If already working in the graphing submenu, steps 1 and 2 below need not be repeated.

1. Type / (Menu) .... /
2. Type G (Graph) .... G
3. Type N (Name) .... N
4. Type C (Create) C
5. ENTER .... ⏎
6. Type graph name.
7. ENTER .... ⏎

Printing Graphs

1. Return to Ready Mode.

2. Type / (Menu .... **/**

3. Type Q (Quit) .... **Q**

4. Type Y (Yes) .... **Y**

5. Type P (Printgraph) .... **P**

6. Remove System Disk from Drive A.

7. Place PrintGraph Disk into Drive A.

8. ENTER .... **↵**

9. Type S (Select) .... **S**

10. Highlight a graph to be printed.

11. Depress space bar to mark the graph for printing. A symbol will be entered next to the selected graph.

12. Repeat steps 10 and 11 for each graph selection.

11. ENTER .... **↵**

12. Type A (Align) .... **A**

13. Type G (Go) .... **G**

14. Type Q (Quit) .... **Q**

Sorting Data

Primary and secondary

1. Type / (Menu) .... **/**

2. Type D (Data) .... **D**

3. Type S (Sort) .... **S**

4. Type D (Data-Range) .... **D**

5. Move cursor to the first item in the data range. (The data range does NOT include field names)

6. Type . (Period) to lock in the range .... **.**

7. Highlight the ENTIRE range of data.

8. ENTER .... **↵**

9. Type P (Primary-Key) .... **P**

10. Place cursor on the first piece of data in the column to be sorted.

11. ENTER .... **↵**

12. Select the sorting order .... Option
    A (Ascending)
    D (Descending)
    A D

13. ENTER .... **↵**

14. Type S (Secondary-Key) .... **S**

15. Repeat steps 10-13.

16. Type G (Go) .... **G**

30

Logical Functions

1. Place cursor in the cell where the answer should appear.

2. Type @ ("at" Symbol) .... `@`

3. Type IF .... `IF`

4. Type ((Open Parenthesis) .... `(`

5. Type the condition to be met.

6. Type , (Comma) .... `,`

7. Type the argument if the condition is true.

8. Type , (Comma) .... `,`

9. Type the argument if the condition is false.

10. Type) (Closed Parenthesis) .... `)`

11. ENTER .... `⏎`

Exiting/Quitting 1-2-3

1. Type / (Menu) .... `/`

2. Type Q (Quit) .... `Q`

3. Type Y (Yes)....................................... `Y`

Getting Help

1. Depress F1 (Help) .... `F1`

Index